Old Mallaig, Morar and Arisaig
Guthrie Hutton

Landing fish at Mallaig in the early 1930s.

© Guthrie Hutton, 2012
First published in the United Kingdom, 2012,
by Stenlake Publishing Ltd.
www.stenlake.co.uk
01290 551122

ISBN 9781840336016

The publishers regret that they cannot supply
copies of any pictures featured in this book.

Arisaig viewed from the road to Rhu.

Acknowledgements

I first saw Mallaig in the early 1960s after travelling overnight from Stornoway on the *Loch Seaforth*. It's a journey that I was never able to repeat, but have been back to the area many times since by rail or road, to work, to visit people and to compile this little book. With every visit a little bit more knowledge was stored away and I must thank the many people who, perhaps inadvertently, contributed to that. My sister gave me invaluable help in this latest venture and I must thank her and the staff at Fort William Library who helped me to carry out research. I must also acknowledge the many people who created an invaluable store of information by setting up numerous web sites.

Further Reading

Atkinson, Tom, *Roads to the Isles*, 1983.
Duckworth, C. and Langmuir, G., *West Highland Steamers*, 1967.
Gifford, John, *The Buildings of Scotland: Highlands and Islands*, 1992.
Haldane, A. R. B., *New Ways Through the Glens*, 1962.
Johnson, Christine, D*evelopments in the Roman Catholic Church in Scotland 1789-1829*, 1983.
Maclean, Loraine, *Discovering Inverness-shire*, 1988.
McGregor, John, *100 Years of the West Highland Railway*, 1994.
Miers, Mary, *The Western Seaboard*, 2008.
Thomas, John, *The West Highland Railway*, 1965.

Introduction

The scenery between Loch nan Uamh and Mallaig must rank as amongst the finest in Scotland, a country replete with scenic splendour. Home to a scattered population, it was a difficult area for outsiders to gain access to. Ships had a long coastline on which to make landfall, but there were no easy natural harbours and large vessels had to stand off, as a French ship did in 1745 when Bonnie Prince Charlie landed on the shore of Loch nan Uamh. His advisers had chosen the spot well as the local clans were staunch Jacobites, and it was from here that the prince set off to garner support and launch his campaign to regain the throne for the Stuarts. He failed and the following year another French ship nosed into the same loch to pick him up, while those he left behind tried to pick up the pieces of their shattered lives.

Prince Charlie's rebellion, and the crackdown that followed it, broke the clan system and as the old order faded, new landlords moved into the area. For some local people this was a positive experience, for others less so. Some enforced evictions and clearances took place and the typical nineteenth century Highland pattern of sheep farming, followed by hunting, shooting and fishing was played out on large estates.

Access to the area remained difficult until, in the early years of the nineteenth century, Arisaig became the destination of a new road pushed westward from Fort William. Then, one hundred years later, this remote spot became one of the best connected in the Highlands when a new railway was driven in from the east. It headed for a bay on the north west tip of North Morar where Lord Lovat, the landlord, had tried fifty years earlier to establish a settlement based on crofting and fishing. There were only a few houses and no proper harbour, but the railway changed all that as the new town of Mallaig became a thriving fishing port and terminal for steamers to and from the islands.

The railway attracted visitors to the area and hotels became established at key places along the line. Tourism developed through the twentieth century, small at first, but increasing over time, but what drew the visitors also attracted the military authorities during the Second World War. A well-connected area, but one that was easy to isolate from prying eyes, was ideal for the most secret of wartime activities.

Before the war was over another of the area's assets, lots of water, made Morar the first place to be developed by the government's new hydro-electric authority. Since then the roads have been greatly improved and the railway has continued to flourish with regular services augmented by heritage steam trains. A heritage centre adjacent to Mallaig Station tells the story to a tourist market that continues to grow. An area that was virtually cut off in the eighteenth century has embraced the many changes that the outside world has thrown at it for two hundred years and turned them to its advantage for the future.

A steam-powered fishing boat from Buckie in Mallaig Harbour.

It was always the intention to build the West Highland Railway to a point on the west coast where a fishing port could be developed to provide profitable freight. Roshven at the mouth of Loch Ailort was initially the favoured option, but, in a classic example of nineteenth century nimbyism, the local landowner forced the railway's promoters to look elsewhere for their harbour. Moidart's loss thus became Mallaig's gain when the search for an alternative led to the bay on the north west tip of North Morar. A breakwater would be needed to make it fit for purpose, but in other respects it was ideal. The station platforms would also have to be protected from the weather by a substantial wall, seen here on the right of a picture showing an early North British Railway train arriving from the east.

Mallaig

The West Highland Railway (Mallaig Extension) Act was passed by parliament in July 1894, but in order to make the line viable another bill was needed to guarantee public money, should a subsidy be needed. It ran into trouble. A Kirkcaldy MP, soured by his experience of the North British Railway Company in Fife, mounted a campaign of opposition. He scuppered the bill, but only until 1896 when it was brought back to parliament and passed. Lady Margaret Cameron of Lochiel cut the first sod at Corpach on 21st January 1897. The parliamentary act allowed 66 months for construction, but well within that deadline, and despite the challenges of Highland weather and difficult terrain, the first trains ran in April 1901. The line had survived the 'Beeching' cuts of the 1960s, and the demise of steam in the same decade when this picture of a diesel-hauled train was taken.

Mallaig

The natural harbour at Mallaig had to be significantly improved to make it suitable for the volume of fish traffic it was expected to handle. The new pier also had to be usable by the large steamers operating connecting passenger services to Skye and Stornoway. Rails were run out along the pier to facilitate the loading or unloading of wagons and fish vans. As anticipated, fish became the railway's main earner, but because the West Highland Railway could not violate the Sabbath, and run trains from Mallaig on a Sunday, the London market found that there were fewer fresh fish on a Monday morning than had been hoped for. In this picture, railway trucks sit on the main pier while the boat in the foreground unloads its catch. Although registered in Belfast it has clear connections with the Isle of Man.

Mallaig

Mallaig was little more than a scatter of houses when it was selected as the railway terminal, but for the people who occupied those houses, the sudden appearance of the modern world on their doorstep must have been an immense shock. If the railway promoters had concerns for them, these would have been well down their list of priorities as they battled to create a railhead on the west coast, but as the harbour and fish trade became established, a sizeable village began to develop. This early picture shows the transition in progress with traditional thatched cottages and the rocky foreshore in the foreground while behind is the new pier lined with railway trucks, and with a steamer alongside.

Mallaig

Planning for the West Highland Railway coincided with the boom years of the herring fishery. Prior to the 1880s herring was not intensively fished by Scots although men from Holland and elsewhere in northern Europe had been basing themselves in Scottish ports and scooping up the silver darlings for their own home markets. When the British developed a taste for herring, the change was rapid and dramatic as large fleets of boats and an army of on-shore workers travelled around the coast chasing the shoals where and when they appeared in season. It was perhaps Mallaig's misfortune that the bonanza peaked only four years after the harbour was opened and declined during and after the First World War. Fishermen everywhere diversified as these men, landing their catch about 1950 have done.

Mallaig

The fishermen in this picture from the 1930s, who look to have caught something larger than herring, also appear to have been working on large east coast boats. A requirement of the British White Herring Act of 1860 was for all fishing boats to have a registration number painted on the bow in white on a black background. It also had to be displayed on a boat's sails or, later, on the funnel. Identifying letters were allocated to each port, which were often the first and last letters of the port name although there were variations, two of which appear here: A for Aberdeen and FR for Fraserburgh. Having been established as a port some time after the act Mallaig did not have registration letters, the closest being OB for Oban, UL for Ullapool and BRD for Broadford on Skye.

Mallaig

With fishing boats from Ballantrae (BA) and Oban in the foreground and others lying five or six deep beside the pier, the harbour looks busy in this picture from 1951. Adding to the activity in the background is the steamer *Lochness*. The third MacBrayne boat to bear the name, she was specifically designed for the service that operated between Mallaig, Kyle of Lochalsh and Stornoway. Launched in June 1929, she made her inaugural run in August that year. She was regarded as handsome rather than pretty, but had good passenger accommodation and a top speed of fourteen knots. She was taken off the run shortly after the end of the Second World War, so the picture may have been taken while *Lochness* was deputising for another vessel.

Mallaig

The ship that replaced *Lochness* on the Mallaig, Kyle of Lochalsh and Stornoway run was the *Loch Seaforth*, seen here on the right. She was ordered from Denny's shipyard at Dumbarton in 1945, but a materials shortage after the Second World War resulted in delays to her construction. Further hold-ups occurred even after her launch in May 1947, so she was not able to make her maiden voyage until December that year. The picture appears to have been taken a few months later, in 1948. With her high bow and squat superstructure she could punch her way across the Minch half an hour faster than *Lochness*. Regular travellers to and from the islands loved her and she remained in service until 1972. By that time new ideas were gaining ground and the route itself was superseded in 1974 when a direct roll-on roll-off ferry service was instituted between Ullapool and Stornoway.

Mallaig

Despite the ending of the Stornoway service, ships of the David MacBrayne, and later Caledonian MacBrayne fleets, have remained a common sight at Mallaig, working to and from the Small Isles, and also Armadale in Skye. The latter is a route that was operated, when this picture was taken in 1956, by Alexander MacLennan (Mallaig) Ltd. using the *Blaven*, the boat sitting at the end of the pier. She was a twin screw motor launch which, between late May and the end of September, did three trips there and back every day, except Sundays. Timings were geared so that the boat linked up with buses running between Armadale and Portree and trains to and from Fort William. An additional evening service was offered in the height of summer.

Mallaig

When Mallaig became a major fishing port some boats were still operating with sails, but steam power was rapidly gaining in popularity. Sailing vessels were always at the mercy of the weather, which could prevent them from getting to the fishing grounds, or worse, hold them at sea with a perishable cargo on board. Steam-driven boats could always make harbour, but once in port they needed to refuel, so coal trains became a familiar sight on the Mallaig railway. Few west coast fishermen could afford the new vessels, so most steam vessels were from the east as this picture of boats from Inverness (INS) and Buckie (BCK) shows. Eventually steam became yesterday's technology and boats were equipped with diesel engines (the Kelvin engine being a particular favourite), so the railway had to deliver oil.

Mallaig

The old pier predated the coming of the railway by some fifty years having been made by Lord Lovat, the local landowner, in an attempt to encourage the growth of a fishing industry at Mallaig. In this early twentieth century picture, some small boats have been drawn up on the shingle beach, beside it. To the left of the pier is a little thatched house, hemmed in by the burgeoning village and looking like something that time forgot. Sitting on the high ground above it is a facility that no self-respecting railway terminal could do without, the Station Hotel. It was built to the designs of architect Duncan Cameron, to coincide with the completion of the railway.

14   **Mallaig**

On a February night in 1927, a fire broke out at the Station Hotel and within twenty minutes the building was a mass of flames that could be seen from the islands. The guest, there was only one, escaped in his night attire, carrying the large sum of money that was in his care, in his role as a commercial traveller. The staff also got out and managed to save some silver and a few items from the front hall. The building was gutted and had to be substantially rebuilt which altered its appearance, as can be seen by comparing this picture from 1932 with the one on the facing page. The hotel was also subsequently renamed the West Highland Hotel. Further up the hill, beyond the hotel, is St. Columba's Parish Church, designed by James G. Falconer and completed by 1903.

Mallaig

The rapid pace in the growth of Mallaig's fishing industry had to be matched by the provision of piers and facilities needed to service the fleet. Some of these can be seen in this view of the village in 1948, with the slipway of one of the boatyards on the left and the chandlery and oil supply business on the right. There are some oil wagons on the pier and a coal lorry; the boats latterly may have run on diesel, but cabin stoves were still coal fired. Mallaig also had an ice factory and curing sheds for turning herrings into kippers, one of the best-known brands being D. A. MacRae's 'Red M' kippers. Although fishing declined over the years Mallaig remained busy with landings of prawns, and the crabs and lobsters gathered by smaller inshore craft.

Mallaig

The word 'Marine' can be clearly seen to the right, in the background of the picture on the facing page. It is more obvious on the right of this picture as the Marine Hotel, which in its early days was a temperance hotel. When this picture was taken in the early 1950s it was run by Alexander MacLennan (Mallaig) Ltd. who also operated the Armadale passenger ferry (see page 12) and provided boat sailings to other destinations including the islands of Eigg and Rhum, Castle Tioram in Loch Moidart and the Five Sisters of Kintail. There were three shop units facing the road on the ground floor of the building, the central one of which was occupied by a branch of the Bank of Scotland. Hotel and bank have co-existed, and expanded somewhat since then.

Mallaig

The tourist who took this photograph in June 1953 appears to have become acutely aware of Mallaig's omnipresent seagulls, presaging the story that would unfold ten years later in Alfred Hitchcock's film *The Birds*. On the left is one of the two shops run by D. & W. MacLean Ltd., which between them sold clothing, footwear, household linens, groceries, hardware and fishing tackle. It has since been replaced by a visitor centre, which, along with a boardwalk and seats has made this locality more tourist-friendly. Facing camera is the National Bank, which had its sign changed a few years later when the National and Commercial Banks amalgamated. It has been changed again since to the Royal Bank of Scotland. For a village of Mallaig's size to be served by the branches of two major banks is an indication of the volume and value of trade that was flowing through the harbour.

In the early 1950s, when this picture was taken, the main road in and out of Mallaig came over the hill and, as Annies Brae and Davies Brae, dropped steeply toward the harbour. The Davies Brae section is seen here with the post office on the left. Next to it, and half hidden by the telephone box, is the shop of Campbell Watt, one of the principal retailers in the village at this time. The sign above the door advertises its role as information point for boat trips, but it was also a newsagent, stationer, tobacconist and confectioner. It sold fruit, fancy goods and toys including Dinky Toys and Meccano and if a child was cut by any of these, Campbell Watt supplied bandages too. There was even a library, a facility that local shops sometimes provided. The steamer *Lochness* can be seen in the background.

Mallaig

The road over the hill was superseded in the late 1980s when a new route in and out of Mallaig was created around the shoreline, enhancing the appearance of the village. In its early days Mallaig gained a reputation as a hotchpotch of unplanned buildings, even as a shanty town, although such a description was probably made more for effect than accuracy. There is no doubt that it was difficult terrain on which to build and this is reflected in the way buildings were positioned. Behind the chickens in the foreground are some council houses, the first of which in Mallaig were formally opened by Lady Hermione Cameron of Lochiel in May 1922. In the central middle distance, close to the shoreline, the highlighted gable ends of some of the original railway housing can be seen. The Island of Skye fills the horizon.

Mallaig

On the right of this early 1950s view, looking north from the high ground to the south of the village, is St Columba's Church with the West Highland Hotel further down the hill. In March 1922 a lightning strike tore a hole in the church roof, damaged the gable wall and blew out windows, including one of stained glass commemorating the wartime sacrifice of men from Mallaig. The blast also broke some hotel windows. The fishing industry is evidently flourishing because smoke can be seen rising from the kippering kilns down at the harbour. By the 1960s fish were being transported by road, rather than rail. Heavily loaded lorries had a hard job climbing the hill out of the village and with liquid from their cargo pouring out behind them, often turned the road into a slippery slope.

Mallaig didn't end with the buildings in the vicinity of the pier, but continued around East Bay to Courtechan, the direction in which these three women are walking. It's a curious picture because usually a photographer would want his subjects to face camera with a smile, but here they are walking purposefully away. The women appear to be fisher lassies, one of the groups of itinerant workers who followed the herring fleets as they migrated around the coasts of Britain. As the season usually started in the Hebrides many of these girls came from the islands. They had to find temporary accommodation wherever they went, so this group were probably heading for their lodgings. Since the early 1920s, when this picture was taken, there has been considerable housing development 'round the bay'.

Mallaig

It would be reasonable to assume that Mallaigvaig (Mallaig Bheag: little Mallaig) is so named because it is smaller than the main port, but actually Mallaigmore (big Mallaig) is further to the east, around the large headland in the background of this early twentieth century picture. Facing Loch Nevis, Mallaigvaig is a more sheltered harbour than the railway port, and an older settlement site. When Bonnie Prince Charlie came back to the mainland from Skye, he made landfall at Mallaigvaig before making his way back to Loch-nan-Uamh. If he could have seen the future, he might have found it just a little ironic that one of the main tourist attractions in the area where he was being so mercilessly hunted, was a train named *The Jacobite*.

Mallaigvaig

The Mallaig road sweeps across the foreground of this view, takes a sharp bend around the cemetery on the left and heads east toward the village of Morar. A motorbike is parked at the roadside near to the telegraph pole and because there is no obvious reason for it to be there, the probability is that it belonged to the photographer. A favourite trick of early photographers was to 'dress' a picture with their own vehicle, to add foreground interest, but here the view is sufficiently splendid to obviate the need for such a tactic. If the theory is correct it provides an insight into the life of postcard photographers, biking round the country looking for saleable views. The road featured in the picture has since been superseded by a new one that runs along the shoreline and Morar village has expanded considerably.

The Mallaig and District Games caused such disruption on the narrow road when they were originally held at Mallaig, that they were moved to Morar where this picture was taken in August 1930. The weather was dull, but rain only started to fall in the last hour, so the unfurled umbrellas suggests that the picture was taken late in the day. Dancers appear to be preparing to strut their stuff on the podium, possibly in the exhibition dance for which a special prize was awarded to the three competitors. R. Cuthbertson took most of the dancing honours. Another outstanding performer was W. Barrie from Glasgow who won the two open piping classes. The rest of the programme was made up of the usual Highland Games events of running, throwing, caber tossing and wrestling, with the added fun of a pillow fight: D. MacDonald of Mallaig beat J. MacDonnell of Bracora in that one.

The promoters of the West Highland Railway thought that Mallaig should only be used for trains and boats, because the land surrounding their terminal was too rocky and uneven for a habitable village to be developed. Instead they thought that Morar, with its more level ground, would make a suitable village site, but despite the existence of a station at Morar, such an idea was never going to catch on. Nevertheless a village did start to develop with at its heart a large and imposing hotel adjacent to the station. It is seen in this picture, which was used as a postcard in 1908 by someone who found it a 'lovely district' helped by 'perfect weather'. They also enjoyed boat trips and a railway excursion to Glenfinnan.

Morar

In the half-century that elapsed between the picture on the facing page being taken and this one, Morar grew into a sizeable village, although the expanded hotel is still prominent, as is the station in the foreground. To the right is a single railway carriage that could be a camping coach. The idea of converting old passenger carriages into holiday accommodation, and parking them at suitable locations, was first tried by the London and North Eastern Railway Company (LNER) in 1933. The West Highland Railway had become part of the LNER ten years earlier when all of Britain's railways were amalgamated into four large companies and these were nationalised as British Railways in 1948. They revived the camping coach idea in 1952, basing one vehicle at Morar. It arrived in the spring and its departure for maintenance marked the end of the season.

Morar

Although Morar is small, its name has become widely known for a number of reasons, although top of the list must be the white sands. They feature in all the tourist brochures, but because printed photographs (or even pictures on web sites) never quite convey the stunning whiteness, nothing can fully prepare a visitor for one of the finest scenic spectacles in Scotland. The sands are white because they are quartz rich, having been ground out of the local schists (metamorphic rocks) by the huge glacier that formed the cleft now filled by Loch Morar. Millions of years ago, as the glacier inched forward it pushed the finely ground rock particles ahead of it, depositing them on the Morar shore. The picture looks across the Morar estuary from the old road on the east side of the bay.

Morar

The West Highland Railway's Mallaig extension had to be driven through some very difficult terrain on a tight budget. Much of the rock along the route was tough and unworkable, and therefore useless for masonry construction, but Robert McAlpine, the contractor who won the job, would make light of these disadvantages. Known as 'Concrete Bob' he was an advocate of the relatively new medium of mass concrete which was cheaper to build and maintain than iron and stone, and could also use the local rock as aggregate. He built some spectacular concrete viaducts one of which was a 90 foot span over the River Morar. This picture shows its underside with the pattern of shuttering clearly visible. McAlpine also based his workforce at a number of camps along the route, one of which was at Morar.

Morar

In 1943 Tom Johnston, the Secretary of State for Scotland in Winston Churchill's wartime cabinet, piloted the legislation through parliament that set up the North of Scotland Hydro-Electric Board. The following year the board announced its first proposals, one of which was a scheme to harness the power of the Morar River. It was opened just before Christmas, 1948, on the same day as another small scheme at Lochalsh, but Morar was first because it was opened in the morning. Paraffin lamps were used to light the ceremony, which was performed by Mrs. Catherine Mackenzie, a widow who still worked the croft where she was born. She spoke in Gaelic: 'gun tigeadh solus agus neart gus na croitean (let light and power come to the crofts)' and then operated the control handle to switch on the lights. The power station, hewn out of the rock and partially underground, is seen here along with other pictures of the spectacular Falls of Morar.

Morar

The top end of the River Morar is seen here in the late 1930s, about ten years before the hydro-electric dam raised the water level by about three feet. It was always a short river, but the raised level had the effect of making it shorter and look more like the end of the loch than the start of the river. Behind some trees on the river bank is the Church of Our Lady and St. Cumin. Built in 1889, and with a distinctive round tower at one corner, it continues Morar's strong Catholic tradition. Following the Reformation of 1560 strictures were imposed on Catholicism and reinforced in 1700 by a thoroughly intolerant Act of the Scottish Parliament aimed at 'preventing the growth of Popery'. Attitudes began to soften through the rest of the eighteenth century and, with the passing of the Scottish Catholic Relief Act of 1793 and the Emancipation Act of 1829, Catholics were able to build their own churches and worship more openly.

Morar was a Catholic, and therefore a staunch Jacobite area, largely because the clan chiefs, the MacDonalds of Glengarry, were Catholic. Simon Fraser, Lord Lovat, who bought the clan lands in 1768, was also a Catholic. The Lovat family did much to improve their estates and were responsible for building the church on the facing page and Morar Lodge, the house in this picture. Initially erected in 1878, it is seen here after being extended to the right of the central chimney. From a high vantage point, the lodge looks south across Loch Morar and the cluster of islands at its western end. One of these, Eilean Ban, was the location of a little seminary that was abandoned after it attracted unwelcome attentions from government soldiers following the Jacobite Rebellions.

Morar

The small crofting community of Bracora occupied a stunning location high above the northern shore of Loch Morar, to the east of Morar Lodge. It is seen here about 1900 some time before it was deserted. Loch Morar, on the right, is remarkable in many ways. Steeped in legend and folklore it is the reputed home of Morag, the local rival to the Loch Ness Monster. At over 1,000 feet to the bottom, it is the deepest loch in Scotland and only second in Europe to a Norwegian fjord. Fishing for sea trout and salmon was popular on Loch Morar and a fish ladder was made to ensure that the hydro-electric dam did not obstruct the passage of fish on the river. Crofters could augment their income by acting as ghillies and some small boats used for fishing parties, can be seen at the river's edges in the picture on page 31.

Bracora, Loch Morar

The road along the northern side of Loch Morar peters out beyond Bracora, at Bracorina. It clearly went further at one time, but time and the elements have reduced it to a rough path (at least they had before a bad ankle meant that your scribe could no longer take this favourite walk). Swordland Lodge, about four miles east of Bracorina, was still occupied in the 1960s by unlikely rebels, an elderly couple who refused to pay rates to Inverness County Council because they got no services. After another half mile, the track swings left to Tarbet on Loch Nevis, which, like all other places in Scotland with similar names, is at a narrow neck of land between two bodies of water. The track between the lochs is seen here in 1937 along with another picture that shows the little boat from Mallaig that served communities on Loch Nevis and Inverie on Knoydart.

Tarbet, Loch Nevis

The pictures on the facing page were taken by a group of women on holiday in a cottage, in the steadings at Glenancross Farm near Morar. They are seen here taking breakfast outside, which, had it been on the terrace of a Monte Carlo hotel might have had a certain cachet, but to do it on the cobbles of a Morar farm steading must have taken a certain kind of jolly stoicism. Having eaten they then washed up in a basin, which suggests there was no running water, although the big iron frying pan would have been of little use without a kitchen range and a hot fire. The Morar hydro-electric plant was still a decade away, so there would have been no electric light, only paraffin lamps or candles. Holiday expectations were different then and coping with such inconveniences would have been part of the fun.

Morar

Glenancross was a nineteenth century farmhouse with steadings flanking a courtyard. Its proximity to the sea made it a delightful place for a holiday, and our ladies evidently enjoyed going to the beach for bathing and picnics. One of them took this picture of the farm from the track that led to and from the shore. The main Mallaig to Fort William road is seen passing the gate, part of which was described in the *SMT Magazine* of October 1936 as being 'positively dreadful'. With such a recommendation, it was not busy when this picture was taken, but increased traffic in the second half of the twentieth century resulted in the old road being by-passed. Much of the traffic growth came from people using holiday accommodation that has improved in quantity and quality since the intrepid ladies stayed at the farm. In the background, to the left of the farm, is Garramor House.

Morar

Built in the nineteenth century as a shooting lodge, Garramor House was one of a number of large houses in the area taken over during the Second World War for training people in 'ungentlemanly warfare'. Here the Special Operations Executive instructed agents, who were to be sent behind enemy lines, in the delicate arts of deception, subterfuge and killing. After the war the house was taken over by the Scottish Youth Hostels Association. The SYHA had been formed in February 1931 and by the outbreak of war had established a network of hostels around the country. Usually fitted out with dormitories and common cooking facilities, the hostels encouraged young people to travel the country cheaply and safely. Its years as a hostel ended after the new road was built and Garramor House became a small hotel.

Morar

The Gaelic for beach is 'traigh' and so Traigh Beach, seen here with a small boat anchored to the shore, is a linguistic confusion that in effect means Beach Beach (or Traigh Traigh). Traigh House could equally be translated as Beach House, which has a slightly downmarket ring to it for such a grand building. Originally known as Morar House, it was built in 1784, although the gabled frontage on the right dates from the early twentieth century. Like Garramor, Traigh House was used by the Special Operations Executive as a base for the training of agents during the Second World War. Amongst the growing number of tourist facilities along this coast, is a nine hole golf course adjacent to Traigh House. It is regarded as beautiful and testing, although focusing on the game, rather than the scenery, could well be one of the biggest challenges.

Traigh

With mobile devices so much part of the modern world, it's hard to understand how important a little communications hub, like this one at Back of Keppoch, was to a remote community. Between them the post box and telephone box opened up the outside world. Red telephone boxes went through a number of design and construction phases before they were installed throughout the country after the mid-1930s. In places of scenic value, like this, the bright red was often regarded as intrusive and a compromise of grey body with red glazing bars was permitted, although such sensitivities soon disappeared as people grew to love the red boxes. Both telephone and post boxes have been replaced by modern versions, although an old red one decorates the hotel across the road. The pecking chickens in the foreground and cultivation strips on the low ground beyond are indicative of a crofting community.

Back of Keppoch

Back of Keppoch's crofting credentials are clear in this early twentieth century view. The little thatched house is typical of a type widely regarded as a traditional crofter's dwelling. Such buildings appear throughout the Highlands and Islands and while superficially they all look alike there were often regional differences. In this one the walls are neatly built, with a gentle batter and stonework that appears almost to be coursed. Unlike some Hebridean houses, where the thatch sits inside the wall head, here it overlaps the wall and is held down with a tidy criss-cross pattern of ropes, another aspect of these buildings that varies widely. The other houses, with square walls, slate roofs and chimneys may look more modern, but there was a long overlap between the time when the building of such houses began and the old ones stopped.

Back of Keppoch

The scatter of houses and outbuildings in this picture of Arisaig, shows that crofting was carried out here before the modern world presented people with other opportunities. The most obvious intrusion was the railway, but before that a road was built in the early years of the nineteenth century to link Arisaig with Fort William. Concerned about Highland depopulation, the government of the day set up a body known as the Commissioners for Highland Roads and Bridges whose remit was largely spelled out in their title. Their engineer, Thomas Telford, identified routes and drew up specifications, and of the many roads that he planned, the one to Arisaig was first. Work started in 1804, but it didn't go smoothly. The contractors from Perth underestimated the difficulties of terrain and weather, but so too did Telford and the road took considerably longer to complete than expected. The modern road that has superseded it would occupy the foreground if this picture were to be replicated today.

Arisaig

When the West Highland Railway opened between Queen Street Station in Glasgow and Fort William in 1894 it did so with new locomotives specially designed for the line by the operating company, the North British Railway. They were relatively light, yet strong enough to deal with moderate weights on a curving, hilly track that didn't allow for a great turn of speed. These same engines were used on the Mallaig extension when it opened and one can be seen here at Arisaig early in the life of the line. The passenger coaches were also specially designed for the line with large windows and an internal layout that gave the maximum number of passengers a good view. Between the carriages and the locomotive are three fish wagons, which would be at the end of the train, loaded with fish, on the return journey.

Arisaig

In the picture on the facing page Arisaig Station is shown in a view that looks east to the mountains of Moidart and in this view it is seen looking west toward the island of Eigg. Unusually for the single track West Highland Railway there are two platforms and double tracks, because Arisaig was timetabled as a crossing point where trains going east and west could pass each other. If a train going in either direction was late, it held up the other which had to wait until the tablet that allowed a train to proceed onto a section of track had been handed over. The signal box on the left was, like the others on the line, made of wood and supplied by the company that installed the signalling while the station buildings were of concrete construction and built to a standard West Highland design.

Arisaig

While battling the tough terrain and often tougher weather, the one advantage the railway builders had was access to the sea and ships to bring in materials. The proximity to water is clear from this picture of the village taken from the station in the early 1930s. It is a difficult view to replicate because the modern road runs straight through the middle between station and village. The railway not only helped to attract new people to the area it brought employment and this, along with estate work, was one reason for the early demise of crofting as a major activity. There was no fishing or any other industry, but that did not stop Arisaig from developing into a proper village, with a village hall, shops, schools and churches. The belfry of the early nineteenth century Church of Scotland can be seen silhouetted against the loch in the centre of the picture.

Arisaig

When ships were used to transport heavy goods and bulk cargoes, Arisaig Pier, situated at Rhu, served the surrounding area, but that traffic had ceased by the mid-twentieth century leaving the water to small pleasure craft. This boat, being rowed by children, has taken to the waters of Loch nan Ceall under the watchful eye of a responsible adult, although quite what he would have done when the children got away from the shore is anyone's guess. Another kind of boating activity that continued after the demise of commercial shipping was the operation of pleasure cruises to the island of Eigg, allowing visitors to get a close-up view of the extraordinary hill, An Sgurr. It formed when lava poured into a valley before becoming solid rock, a columnar pitchstone. The original valley has eroded away to leave the feature which rises to a height of nearly 1,300 feet and gives the island its distinctive profile.

Arisaig

Loch nan Ceall, fringed with silver sand, flanked by Keppoch and Rhu, and with its entrance partly enclosed by rocks and islets is glorious. Distant views of the Small Isles and a backdrop of hills add to a superb scenic mix that, even before the road and rail developments gave tourism extra impetus, had been drawing people to the area. With mid-eighteenth century origins, many of those visitors will have stayed at the Arisaig Hotel, seen here nestling below a bank of higher ground. The Island of Eigg can be seen on the horizon, so it's a fair bet that a few guests will have joked about having an egg for breakfast. Some visitors to the area, Czechoslovakian freedom fighters who trained here during the Second World War, have been honoured with a memorial erected beside the loch shore at Arisaig.

Arisaig

Arisaig was part of the fiefdom of the Macdonalds of Clanranald, but the breakdown of the clan system after the 1745/46 Jacobite uprising ended with these clan lands being lost. The principal culprit was the 20th chief who led a dissolute lifestyle and ran up debts that could only be met by selling off chunks of his estate. Arisaig passed through the hands of a couple of owners before it was acquired in the mid-nineteenth century by Francis Astley who carried out many improvements and proved to be a better laird than the last Clanranald. Following in his footsteps, his heir, Constance Astley, built Faire na Sgurr at the start of the twentieth century. Described by a contemporary casual observer as an 'open air treatment house', it was sited on the Strath of Arisaig to make the most of the sun and fresh air, ideal for people who suffered from tuberculosis, of which Miss Astley was one.

Arisaig

Arisaig House was designed by the architect Philip Webb and built for Francis Astley in 1863/64, but a disastrous fire in September 1935, that occurred soon after this picture was taken, all but destroyed it. The house was let at the time to shooting tenants who were woken by the sound of a bell that had begun to ring because of the action of flames. They all escaped and some items of furniture and silver were saved, but with no adequate means of getting water onto the blaze it had to be left to burn itself out. By 1937 Miss C. G. Astley-Nicholson had rebuilt the house, although slightly smaller and with the loss of some of its visual appeal. Such considerations did not weigh too heavily on the minds of the Special Operations Executive who took the house over during the Second World War as the headquarters for training people in the skills of clandestine warfare. It was from here that the activities carried out at Garramor, Traigh and a number of other big houses in the area were co-ordinated.

Arisaig